GW00746652

Gluten-free

Dairy-free

A SIMPLE GUIDE

An introduction to healthy
cooking without wheat, milk,
cheese or other common
allergens

Caroline Osborne

First published in Great Britain 2015
by Rethink Press (www.rethinkpress.com)

© Copyright Caroline Osborne

All rights reserved. No part of this publication may be reproduced, stored in or introduced into a retrieval system, or transmitted, in any form, or by any means (electronic, mechanical, photocopying, recording or otherwise) without the prior written permission of the publisher.

The right of Caroline Osborne to be identified as the author of this work has been asserted by her in accordance with the Copyright, Designs and Patents Act 1988.

This book is sold subject to the condition that it shall not, by way of trade or otherwise, be lent, resold, hired out, or otherwise circulated without the publisher's prior consent in any form of binding or cover other than that in which it is published and without a similar condition including this condition being imposed on the subsequent purchaser.

Illustrations © Hamilton Wilson

Contents

Introduction

More and more people are finding that food intolerances are to blame for their health problems, both minor and major. The range of symptoms that might be caused by food intolerances is huge, and includes headaches, nausea, bloating, diarrhoea or constipation, colitis, itching and rashes, lethargy, depression, irritability and insomnia. These seemingly unconnected symptoms, while not necessarily life-threatening, definitely threaten quality of life. (A food allergy, as opposed to an intolerance or sensitivity, is much more serious and can be life-threatening.)

The rapid relief from nagging discomforts makes it really worth the effort to give up eating certain foods – and it is an effort. By a quirk of nature, we're actually addicted to the foods that we can't digest properly. The immune system produces a drug-like substance in response to foods it has learned to treat as foreign bodies.

The commonest culprits are gluten and cow's milk, with maize, soya, eggs and nightshades also being problem foods for many people. (The nightshades family of plants includes potatoes, tomatoes, peppers, aubergines – and tobacco.)

It seems terribly unfair that those foods that are staples in our diet are the very ones that people become sensitive to. However, it's because they are so prevalent in the western diet that they become problems. On a normal diet, we're constantly consuming wheat, milk, cheese, potatoes and tomatoes. They're in almost every processed food in some form or other. Maize (often as cornmeal) is used as a thickener in many tinned soups, gravy powders etc. Soya is not only used in many vegetarian foods, but is also added to bread to increase the protein content (to make up for what they've taken out in processing the flour!). This means that we need always to read the label very carefully when buying ready-made foods, if we want to avoid these ingredients.

Celiac disease is a special case of food intolerance, where a person has an inborn metabolic inability to digest proteins contained in gluten. These people may also have a secondary intolerance to the lactose in milk products, and maybe to other foods. This is due to damage to the digestive tract caused by gluten. The secondary intolerances can clear up as the digestive tract heals on a gluten-free diet.

As gluten intolerance becomes more widely recognised, more and more gluten-free products are appearing on the market, including books on gluten-free cooking. Supermarkets usually now have a 'free-from' section. Most of these products and books assume that people generally have sensitivity to only one food, whereas, in fact, people with food sensitivities often have several different foods they need to avoid. Potato flour is used a lot in ready-made gluten-free products and in mixtures sold as gluten-free flour. Ready-made gluten-free foods also usually contain additives such as preservatives, emulsifiers, colours and flavours. Books on gluten-free cooking often use potato flour in their recipes, and frequently have cheese or milk as ingredients as well. Milk intolerance is probably at least as common as gluten intolerance. (Anyone who has asthma, frequent colds, waxy ears or other mucous problems would do well to try eliminating milk and milk products from their diet.)

PICKING HAZELNUTS

This book assumes that anyone who is sensitive to gluten might also have to avoid dairy products, soya and nightshades, and possibly eggs and maize as well. Its aim is to teach you to cook confidently with the many natural wholefoods which are alternatives to wheat, dairy, maize etc.

You'll feel so much better not only because you're no longer eating foods your body is fighting against, but also because you are in charge of your food, and of your health. By preparing your own food from basic ingredients you have total control over what goes into it – no unwanted allergens, no preservatives or other additives. It needn't take a lot of time and it's far more satisfying than buying ready-made foods – and can be much more fun!

Adapting Traditional Recipes

There is no need to throw away your old recipe books. Many recipes are gluten-free and dairy-free anyway. Where a recipe does call for something you can't eat, there's nearly always a suitable substitute. Learn to be creative and daring with your recipes – it's your kitchen, do it your way.

Look through your recipe books and note which recipes you can use as they are. Then go through the rest and work out what substitutes you need to use in each recipe. The following pages will guide you in finding substitutes that work for you. Further on is an introduction to gluten-free grains and how they can be used to substitute for wheat, oats, etc. The recipes in this book should give you a good start to home baking without gluten, and some ideas to help you give up dairy products.

Most salads don't have gluten in any form – but be careful of ready-made salad dressings – wheat and milk products find their way into many foods, so read the label carefully before you buy. For pasta salads and other pasta dishes, gluten-free pastas are available in health food shops. These are usually made from corn (maize), rice or buckwheat. Rice salads and other rice dishes should be fine as they are.

Casseroles and gravies often call for wheat flour as a thickener. Instead use corn flour (if you can eat maize), rice flour (not quite such a good thickener), arrowroot (good) or kuzu (the best, but expensive). Alternatively, puréed vegetables work very well. Parsnips and sweet potatoes are particularly good for this. For a thick stew or casserole, at the end of the cooking take out some of the vegetables and some of the liquid and purée in a blender or food processor, or mash with a fork. Stir back into the rest of the dish.

Many people worry that they won't get enough calcium if they don't eat milk and cheese. This isn't true: milk is not a good source of calcium as the calcium in pasteurised milk and cheese is not in a form that can be easily absorbed by the body, and many people can't digest milk anyway.

On the other hand, vegetables are a very good source of calcium as calcium is the principle mineral in plants. Cows get all the calcium they need from grass! Nuts and seeds too are very rich in calcium. The calcium in plants is in a form that we can easily assimilate.

However, it's not always easy to give up milk. I admit that I found it very difficult to give up milk products at first, especially cheese. It took me several years of being off and on before I'd completely eliminated them from my diet. If you're finding it hard, take heart: it gets easier the longer you stick to it. It helps to have substitutes for the dairy products that are a regular part of your diet. There are substitutes for milk and butter that work reasonably well in most cases. For spreading, use a non-hydrogenated, dairy-free vegetable margarine instead of butter. These are available from health food shops – most supermarket margarines contain milk in some form, usually whey. Or try coconut oil. This is a spreadable consistency at normal room temperatures, tastes only mildly of coconut and is incredibly good for you.

If you have a problem digesting milk, you might find that you can still use butter, as it doesn't contain any of the milk proteins or sugars. In cooking, water can often be used instead of milk, and oil, dairy-free margarine or coconut oil instead of butter. Quiche can be made without milk, using water and extra eggs instead. Always use good quality, cold-pressed oil. Extra-virgin olive oil is the best for most cooking and generally for salad dressings. Sunflower oil is lighter and is usually more suitable for baking. Coconut oil is also excellent for baking as it's very stable at high temperatures and isn't damaged by heat.

There are soya-based substitutes for milk, cheese, yoghurt and cream. While some of these are very tasty, I don't recommend soya products other than the traditional fermented ones (i.e. tofu, tempeh, soy sauce and miso). Unfermented soya interferes with calcium absorption and mimics oestrogen, so it upsets your normal hormone balance.

Where a milk substitute is needed for drinks or to have with breakfast cereals, there are alternatives readily available, even in supermarkets, such as rice milk and oat milk. Nut milk can be made at home (see recipe in Milk and Cheese Substitutes section).

Non-dairy yoghurt substitutes are available in health food shops. These are generally soya based, so are not really a good idea. A new product is a yoghurt substitute made from coconut oil, which is both delicious and healthy.

A delicious alternative to sour cream can be made with cashew nuts.

Cheese is much harder to replace, but not impossible. I have a recipe for 'Nut Cheese' that makes a delicious and healthy alternative for soft cheeses. Tofu can sometimes be used as a substitute for cheese – for instance, in place of feta cheese in Greek salads.

Dips and spreads are often based on cream cheese but there are many that are dairy-free. Hummus is dairy-free, and can be made without tahini (sesame paste) for those who can't eat sesame seeds. Many brands of hummus available in shops leave out the tahini because so many people are allergic to sesame seeds.

Dips and spreads can be made from beans, or from vegetables, raw or cooked, flavoured with herbs and spices (see recipe for Spicy Sweet Potato Dip). The recipe for Nut Cheese makes a very tasty spread or dip.

Soups that are pure vegetable are usually ok. Soups called 'cream of... ' will have milk or cream in the recipe. To get a similar colour and texture, add parsnip, swede or cooked butterbeans and puree until really smooth. A bit of creamed coconut adds richness to vegetarian soups and makes a satisfyingly creamy texture. Or add some nut milk.

Nightshades include a wide range of different vegetables, requiring different strategies to replace them. Potatoes, tomatoes, chilli peppers, sweet peppers and aubergines are all nightshades, as are cayenne pepper and tobacco.

Potatoes can be very hard to give up; they've become such a staple in the western diet that it's hard to imagine life without them. However, there are many other vegetables that can take their place. Our ancestors used swede, turnip and parsnip long before the Spanish brought potatoes over from America. Parsnip and swede mashed together (mashed 'neaps') make a very tasty substitute for mashed potatoes and can be used in shepherd's pie or any other meal in place of mashed potatoes. Swede, parsnip, carrots, squash and sweet potato can often be used instead of potatoes, whether you want them boiled, mashed, roasted, as chips or in soups or stews.

Tomatoes are a unique and versatile food (they are actually fruit not vegetable), and can be used raw in salads and sandwiches or cooked in soups, stews, casseroles and sauces. They are possibly the hardest food to find a substitute for.

If you miss tomato in salads, be adventurous and try other fruits. Avocados are good in salads, but you could also try peach or nectarine, or kiwi fruit. These fruits could also be used in sandwiches, or try pureed, raw carrot or sweet potato as a sandwich spread.

Tomatoes add richness to both the colour and the flavour of soups, stews and sauces. Try replacing them with puréed carrots with a little beetroot for colour.

Eggs have unique properties, whether used in baking or raw as an emulsifier as in mayonnaise. However, there are egg replacers available in health food shops, which can be used for baking. Egg-free mayonnaises are also available in health food shops. (Try to avoid the soy-based ones.)

Gluten-Free Grains

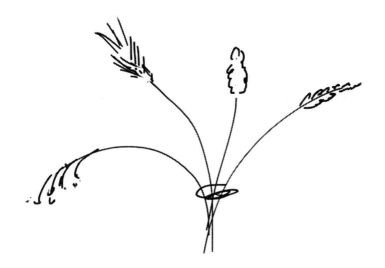

A word on gluten

Gluten is found in wheat, barley, rye and (to a lesser extent) oats. Wheat has the most gluten. Gluten is the 'glue' that holds flour together. It is what enables bread to rise and also gives dough its elasticity. This is what makes wheat flour so (relatively) easy to work with, and is why wheat is used so much. Most baked products available in the supermarkets are made from wheat flour – so much so that the word 'flour' on its own listed in the ingredients implies (white) wheat flour.

There are two ancient forms of wheat still grown today which some people can safely use who can't eat modern wheat. Spelt was used in Roman times and is available in shops today as flour and sometimes as a whole grain. Kamut was used in ancient Egypt. Both spelt and kamut have less gluten than modern wheat.

And non-gluten

There are many other grains and flours which don't contain any gluten. The best known of course is rice, but there are several others readily available in health food shops. Among these are buckwheat, quinoa, millet, gram flour, amaranth and maize. Maize (corn) though gluten free, is a common allergen. Gram flour is made from a type of chickpea. Flour can also be made from other pulses, from roots such as potato, tapioca, and cassava; and from nuts such as chestnuts or almonds. As mentioned above, ready-made gluten-free products, like ready-made gluten-free flour, often contain potato flour, because it helps to hold things together. Other flours, such as tapioca, do this too, but they aren't as cheap.

Soya is also sold as flour. While it is gluten free, it's not a good idea to use it at all as soya contains toxins and plant oestrogens that disrupt normal hormonal function in humans and animals. Traditional soya products such as soy sauce and tofu are fermented for many months, which reduces these toxins. (Be careful: the cheapest brands of soy sauce are made by a modern, quick process which doesn't involve fermentation – always read the label. If it says 'brewed' or 'aged' the soy sauce has been fermented.)

Wheat and oats are used in forms other than flour, such as couscous and bulgur wheat (cracked wheat) and porridge oats. Gluten free grains can usually be used instead. Millet and quinoa make good substitutes for couscous. Amaranth has a slightly different taste but a similar texture and could also be used in couscous recipes. Quinoa is an excellent substitute for bulgur wheat in Tabouleh salad (see recipe). Rice flakes or millet flakes can be used instead of oats to make muesli or porridge. These flaked grains also make good 'crumble' to top a fruit crumble or a savoury casserole.

CHICKPEAS

To summarise, the glutinous grains are wheat, rye, barley and oats. Spelt, kamut, couscous and bulgur are all forms of wheat.

The gluten-free grains include rice, buckwheat, quinoa, millet, amaranth and maize. All these can be used as flour or as whole grains. Some are available as flakes and several as 'puffed' whole grains, similar to puffed wheat. Examples of other gluten-free flours include gram flour, chestnut flour, other nut meals, kuzu starch and tapioca. A description of the readily available gluten-free grains follows.

Rice

Rice is too well known to need much introduction. Like wheat, it's a type of grass, and has been a staple food in most of Asia for thousands of years. Rice cultivation has shaped the landscape in many countries. Terraces of paddy fields covering the hillsides are an impressive sight. The terraces are created, with an intricate irrigation system, to allow the fields to be flooded for part of the growing season. Presumably wild rice evolved in the flood plains of river valleys.

There are more different types of rice than just long grain and short grain. Most types are available as brown (wholegrain) or white. In India, Basmati is considered to be the best quality rice. Certainly it's easy to cook and very tasty, whether white or brown. If you're feeling more adventurous, red or black rice make dramatic looking dishes. Wild rice is a distant relative of cultivated rice with a much longer, black, grain. As it is rather expensive it is usually used mixed with other varieties – add a small handful to the pot before cooking.

There are several methods of cooking rice. My own favourite way is the covered pot method: put a little oil in the pot, add the rice, stir, then add one and a half to two cups of water per cup of rice. (White rice generally needs less water than brown.) Cover and bring to the boil. Reduce the heat and simmer gently until all the water has been absorbed (from about 15 minutes for white rice to 40 minutes for short grain brown rice). This method works well in a pressure cooker, or a saucepan with a well-fitting lid, so not too much steam escapes.

Rice is also available as flakes, which can be used to make muesli or used instead of oats for porridge. Rice flakes need very little cooking – just pour boiling water over the flakes in a bowl and leave it to soak for a few minutes. Serve it with a pinch of salt, a spoonful of honey, or whatever you normally have with porridge. Rice porridge makes a good baby food, very quick to prepare and easy to digest (don't add salt or any sweetener for babies).

Rice flour is possibly the most useful gluten free flour, though it makes crumbly dough. It doesn't have a strong taste so it's good for sweet or savoury dishes. It's very fine so it's useful for flouring the work surface when rolling pastry.

Quinoa

Quinoa (pronounced 'keenwa') is a small, round 'grain' that comes from the Andes Mountains in South America. It's been cultivated there for at least 5000 years. It was the staple food of the Incas, who called it the 'mother grain'. There are about 1800 varieties today, as each valley has its own type, suited to the specific growing conditions.

Whereas rice, wheat, barley, rye, oats and maize are types of grass, quinoa is actually a fruit. It is high in protein, being about 16% to 20%, compared with wheat at 10% to 14% and rice at 7.5%. Also it has the full complement of amino acids, unlike most grains. (There are 20 essential amino acids that are the 'building blocks' of all protein. Most foods, other than meat and eggs, are short on some or other of the amino acids. This is why meat and eggs are referred to as 'complete proteins'.)

Quinoa is very easily digested and is an alkalising food (see Acidifying and Alkalising Foods). It's very high in iron and has a low glycaemic index.

Quinoa grains have a bitter coating that protects them from birds and insects. This has to be washed off before using it in any recipe, though quinoa sold in health food shops is often pre-washed.

Quinoa can be boiled like rice, though it cooks more quickly – about 10 minutes. Use one to two cups of water to one cup of quinoa, place in a covered saucepan, bring to the boil and simmer for about 10 minutes. Substitute boiled quinoa for rice in any recipe. Quinoa is also available as flakes and as flour. Quinoa flakes can be used to make porridge or muesli, and the flour for all baking purposes.

Millet

Millet originated in South-East Asia, where it has been cultivated for at least 9000 years. It is related to sorghum, which is sometimes called millet. There are actually several related species known as millet, with 6000 varieties grown worldwide today. The plants grow from 2 to 15 feet tall, with grass-like leaves and sprays of densely packed, tiny round seeds. The sprays of seed are often sold as bird food.

While millet is much grown as animal fodder, it has been a staple for humans for thousands of years throughout large parts of the world. It grows easily in dry climates, where there is not enough rain for wheat or barley, and will thrive in poor soils. It grows very quickly, being ready to harvest in 45 to 65 days; and it stores exceptionally well. All of which explain why it has been such an important crop in many parts of the world.

It's traditionally grown in Northern China, Japan, parts of India, Eastern Europe, the Middle East, and North and East Africa. Uses for millet include making flatbreads or noodles from the flour, whole in soups and as a porridge. It has even been used in making beer.

Millet is a very nutritious food, being rich in B vitamins and calcium, iron, magnesium, potassium and phosphorus. It has a similar protein content to wheat, 11% to 15%. Like quinoa, millet is an alkalising food.

Cook the whole grain as for rice or quinoa, allowing 2 to 3 ½ cups of water per cup of millet. It should be light and fluffy when cooked, which takes about 20 minutes, depending on the variety used. Cooked with more water it can become very dense – allow it to cool and slice it as a substitute for bread. For a slightly stronger flavour, roast the grains briefly before cooking. As with quinoa, use in any dish where you would normally use rice. Millet is also available in flakes and can be used in muesli or as porridge. It is sometimes sold as flour

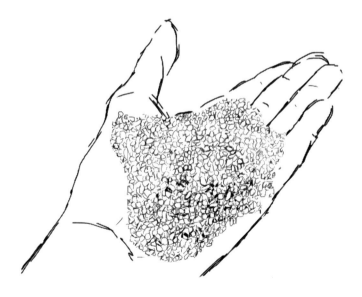

but as it does not keep well in this form it is better to make your own when you need it (use a food mill or coffee grinder). It can also be sprouted, or even popped like popcorn. (Most whole grains can be popped.)

Amaranth

Amaranth (or amarant) was first cultivated in Central and South America over 6000 years ago. There are about 60 species, grown throughout America and large parts of Asia, which are used variously as grain crops, vegetables, ornamentals and dye plants. Amaranths are closely related to the Goosefoot family, which includes pigweed, spinach and beet. 'Love-lies-bleeding' is a type of amaranth from India, grown for ornamental use.

The plants grow to 5 or 6 foot tall with very broad leaves, each plant producing thousands of tiny round seeds. A field of amaranth is very colourful, as the leaves range from maroon through crimson, orange and pink to white, with green as well. The flowers are red or magenta.

Myths about amaranth connect it with immortality because of the long lasting nature of its flowers, even when cut. It was one of the staple foods of the ancient Incas. The Aztecs too cultivated it for food. They also used the seeds, combined with honey and human blood, in religious ceremonies. Because of this, the Spanish invaders forbade the cultivation of amaranth for centuries.

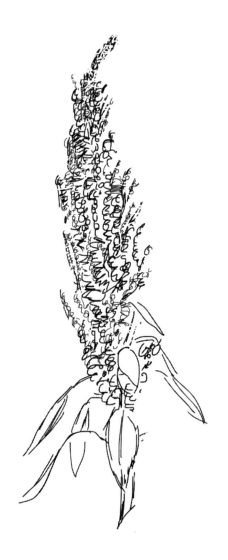

Since the 1970s, amaranth has been making a comeback as a highly nutritious food. The leaves (sometimes known as Chinese spinach) are used as a vegetable in many Asian countries. They are rich in vitamins and minerals. Amaranth seeds are high in protein (15%-18%) and, like quinoa, it has a full complement of amino acids. It has three times the fibre and five times the iron of wheat. It is also high in calcium, potassium and phosphorous and vitamins A and C. Again, like quinoa, it is easy to digest.

Amaranth can be cooked as whole grains by boiling in water. Allow 1½ to 2 ½ cups of water to each cup of amaranth. It can be ground into flour for many uses, including baking, pasta and pancakes. In Mexico the seeds are popped like popcorn and combined with molasses to make a snack. The seeds can also be sprouted.

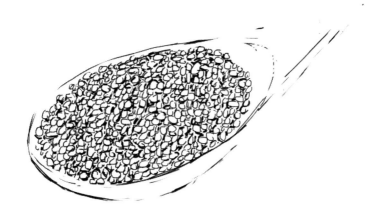

Buckwheat

Buckwheat, though it is often counted as a cereal, is actually not a grass but a broadleaf plant related to dock, sorrel and rhubarb. The name comes from 'beech wheat' as the triangular seeds resemble tiny beechnuts.

Buckwheat was first cultivated at least 6000 years ago in southwest Asia. Its use spread west to Europe and east to central Asia, Tibet and China. It's grown at a higher altitude than any other cultivated plant, on the Tibetan plateau. It grows quickly and does well on poor but well drained soils. Too much fertiliser actually reduces yield. It used to be cultivated in orchards to improve pollination, and it makes a dark, mellow honey. The flowers are sometimes used to make a brown dye.

While the unhulled seeds can be sprouted for eating, the leaves are toxic to humans.

Buckwheat is a very nutritious food. The Chinese army feeds buckwheat to its soldiers to give them stamina and strength. It contains about 12% protein with all eight essential amino acids. (Of the 20 amino acids, 8 cannot ever be made in the human body but must always be obtained from food.) Buckwheat is a good source of vitamin B, potassium and phosphorous, and dietary fibre. It also contains bioflavonoids, including rutin, which is used as a medicine in vascular disorders. It's very low in fat.

It's traditionally used in several forms. Buckwheat flour is grey-brown in colour, with a distinctive, pleasantly earthy flavour. It's often used to make pancakes – called 'blinis' in Russia, 'gallettes' in France. In Holland it is used to make crumpets. In Japan buckwheat flour ('soba') is kneaded with hot water to make dough for noodles. The flour can be used to thicken sauces and soups,

Buckwheat groats are the whole, hulled seeds. These can be cooked as they are (like rice) or roasted first for a slightly sweeter flavour. The groats can be coarsely ground to make 'grits' for porridge-like dishes.

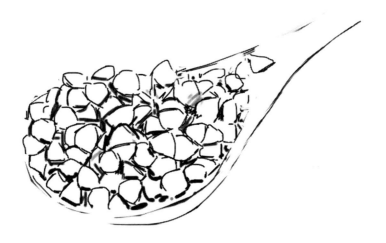

Maize

Maize, or corn, is a cereal grain like wheat. That is, it's a type of grass.

It was first domesticated in Central America and Mexico perhaps 9000 years ago. Cultivation of maize spread north during the first millennium A.D. The Native Americans transformed the landscape, clearing forests to make room for it, in the same way that people cleared the forests of Europe to grow their crops. Maize was a staple food of most pre-Columbian cultures throughout America and the Caribbean. After the European discovery of America in the 15th century use of maize spread further and it's now a major crop in many parts of the world.

Maize looks like a giant grass. In fact some varieties grow to 23 foot (7m) tall, though most commercial varieties grow to only 9 foot (2.5m). We are used to seeing yellow sweetcorn, but maize kernels can be blackish, greyish-blue, red or white as well, often with multiple colours on each cob.

Maize is widely used in many forms. It is used for animal fodder, to make flour, as a vegetable and for popping. Different varieties are grown for different purposes. Sweetcorn varieties used as a vegetable have more sugar and less starch than other types. This is the corn that we buy as corn on the cob, tinned or frozen sweet corn. We are also familiar with maize as cornflakes and as corn flour, used for thickening sauces etc. Cornflour and cornstarch are present in many processed foods, so if you need to avoid corn (maize) be very careful of all processed foods.

It's available as flour in three grades or fineness. The coarsest is maize meal. This is a yellow, grainy meal that's used to make polenta (see recipe, page 57). It's also cooked as porridge (known as 'maize grits'). Maize flour is finer and paler in colour than maize meal. It's used in this form to make traditional Mexican foods such as tortillas. Corn flour is the finest of all and is white. This is familiar to most cooks as the corn flour used to thicken sauces and gravies. Corn flour and cornstarch are used as thickeners in many processed foods. It's because it's so widely used that it has become one of the common food allergens. Also cornstarch is highly processed using bleach and other toxic chemicals. Potato starch is similarly highly processed. Arrowroot and kuzu are naturally produced starches that are excellent thickeners. Both have also been traditionally used as medicine for the digestive system.

Kuzu

Kuzu, or wild mountain root, has been used in China and Japan for at least 2000 years. It's one of the world's largest vegetable roots. Each root grows to two metres (6') length and averages 100kg (200 lb) weight. The top of the plant forms a fast growing, climbing vine.

Kuzu (sometimes spelled kudzu) is revered as both a food and a medicine. The starch is used as a thickening agent in cooking and both the whole root and the starch are used medicinally. It is the first choice in the treatment of digestive disorders, and is also very healing for the liver.

Kuzu starch, or wild mountain root starch, is a fine white powder extracted from the root by a lengthy process that yields only 3kg of starch for every 100kg of root. This makes it comparatively expensive, but it's far superior to any other thickening agent. For anyone with food sensitivities it's a useful addition to the diet because of its healing qualities.

To use kuzu as a thickener, dissolve 1 to 1½ tablespoons of kuzu powder in one cup of cold water or stock and heat gently, stirring all the time, until thick.

Cassava

Cassava is a woody shrub that grows in tropical and sub-tropical regions. The tuberous roots are rich in starch and high in calcium, phosphorous and vitamin C. While the roots are very low in protein, the leaves are protein rich, but need processing to remove toxins.

Cassava is a staple food for approximately 500 million people worldwide, being cultivated throughout Africa, Asia, South America and the Caribbean. It produces more food energy per acre than any other crop (except sugar cane).

The roots can be used as a vegetable or processed to make cassava flour. In Britain it's best known in the form of tapioca pudding. The tapioca sold for making puddings is a flavourless starch reconstituted from cassava root. Tapioca flour is the same as cassava flour. It's a useful addition to gluten free flour mixtures as it helps to make baked foods less crumbly. It can also be used as a thickener for sauces, gravies etc.

Potato Flour

Like cassava, potatoes can be dried and made into flour. This flour is often used in gluten-free mixes because it's cheap and plentiful. Unfortunately potatoes are a problem food for many people with food allergies, which is why I recommend making your own combination of flours to suit your own tastes and needs.

Gram Flour

Gram flour is made from a type of chickpea, dried and ground finely. It has a distinctive sweet flavour. Gram flour is much used in Indian cooking. It's particularly good in batters for fried foods because it doesn't absorb much oil compared to other flours. Other pulses can also be made into flour but gram flour is the most commonly available.

CHICKPEAS

Nuts and Seeds

Many nuts and seeds can be ground finely to make flour, which can be used on its own or added to other flours in many recipes. For instance, I find that the addition of ground sunflower seeds to a gluten-free pastry mixture makes the dough more manageable. Both almonds and chestnuts are commonly used as flour in parts of Europe.

Two seeds that are particularly useful in gluten free baking are flax seeds and chia seeds. They are both hydrophilic, which means they absorb a lot of water – up to 12 times their own weight in the case of chia – forming a thick gel. This helps hold together gluten free dough for pastry or bread.

Flax has been grown in Europe for millennia, both for the fibres to make linen and for the seeds. Chia seeds originally come from Mexico. These tiny greyish seeds are from a plant related to mint, which has been cultivated since Aztec times. It may have been as important as maize as a food crop. Both chia and flax seeds are rich in omega-3 fatty acids

Of course, nuts and seeds cause life-threatening allergic reactions in some people and they must avoid them completely. As we've seen, whatever you have to avoid, there are plenty of substitutes.

PICKING HAZELNUTS

Gums

Xanthan Gum, Guar Gum, Carrageenan Gum, Locust Bean Gum

The problem with gluten free baking is that things don't hold together. One way around this is to use a gum such as Xanthan, guar or carrageenan. These gums act as thickeners and binders.

Gums are used in many commercial foods, not just in gluten free foods. They not only help to hold food together, they also hold a lot of water. This means they can be used as a low-calorie filler, diluting the food with water while keeping it the consistency you'd expect it to have without the extra water. They're often used in ice cream and other dairy products, especially low-calorie versions, and in many diet foods. Not only do they reduce the calories per portion, but they also make you feel full by continuing to soak up water in your stomach. Guar gum is particularly good at this. This can be a problem if you use more than a very small amount, leading to painful bloating. For this reason some of these gums are banned from use in baby foods in some countries.

Carrageenan gum is obtained from red edible seaweeds such as Irish Moss. It's often used as a vegetarian alternative to gelatine. It's been used as a food ingredient for many centuries in Ireland and other countries, though recently there has been some question as to how healthy it is. Some researchers consider it unsuitable for human consumption.

Agar Agar is similar to Carrageenan. It's also made from red seaweeds, and is traditionally used in jellies and similar deserts in Asian cooking.

While seaweeds have always been used as nutritious foods around the world, the extracted gums are used now in more ways and quantities than in traditional use. There seem to be health problems linked with use of Carrageenan and Agar Agar.

Guar Gum, or guaran is made from guar bean, also known as cluster bean, which has been grown for centuries in India and Pakistan. The guar seeds are dehusked, milled and screened to obtain the guar gum, which is usually a free-flowing, whitish powder.

Locust Bean Gum is produced from locust, or carob, beans – the same beans used to make carob flour, often used as a cocoa substitute. Carob beans and the gum produced from them have been in use in food for thousands of years.

Xanthan gum is one of the most commonly used gums commercially. Also called Xantana. Manufacturers advertise it as 'natural' but it's far from being a natural product. It's produced artificially by the action of a bacterium on a source of sugar. The bacterium used is *Xanthomonas campestris,* which gives it its name. This is the bacterium that causes broccoli and other brassicas to go black and slimy. The sugar is typically sourced from cheap food products such as corn, wheat, dairy, or soy. These are all common allergens and the resultant gum will contain traces of these – up to 10%. If you've tried going gluten-free before and didn't find it helped, it could be because of traces of gluten from Xanthan gum in shop-bought 'gluten-free' products.

Xanthan gum has been known to cause health problems for workers in the factories where it's produced. It's not really something you want to add to your diet.

If you're looking out for these ingredients in your shopping, the e numbers for them are:

Agar Agar e406, Carrageenan e407, Guar gum e412, Locust bean gum e410, Xanthan gum e415.

All in all, I can't recommend any of these gums as food ingredients, either for home baking or in bought foods. There are alternatives. Tapioca starch is also very good for helping gluten free breads and pastries hold together. Flax seeds and chia seeds can be ground finely to make a powder with similar properties of water holding and thickening.

Acidifying and Alkalising Foods

The acidity or alkalinity of a substance is measured by its pH, a number between 1 and 14, where 1 is most acid, 7 is neutral and 14 is most alkaline. Blood is slightly alkaline, with a pH of between 7.35 and 7.45. It is vital that it stays within this narrow range.

Muscular activity and most metabolic processes, including the digestion of starches and proteins, lead to an increase in acidity of the blood.

Excess acidity is dealt with in three ways: it's broken down and excreted to a certain extent; it's used up in stomach acid; and it's neutralised by alkalising minerals present in certain foods. Of these three, it is only the third that we have much control over – we can choose to eat more of the alkalising foods. These foods are generally fruits and vegetables, but certain grains are also alkalising, notably quinoa and millet.

If insufficient alkalising minerals are consumed in the diet, these minerals will be taken from stores in the body, leading to problems such as weak teeth and bones. Thus replacing wheat with millet and quinoa has a double benefit: not only removing gluten from your diet, but also increasing the proportion of alkalising to acidifying foods.

Recipes

General Notes
on the Recipes

I personally have to avoid gluten, dairy and nightshades (that
is, potatoes, tomatoes, etc), so these recipes are all gluten free,
dairy free and nightshade free. If you do want to use milk
products, butter can be substituted for oil and milk for water
in some recipes. Cheese can be added where appropriate.
Where a recipe calls for egg I've given an alternative without
egg. I have included a few recipes using maize, but there are
plenty of recipes without maize for people who need to avoid
it. All recipes use only natural ingredients.

Weights are given in metric and Imperial. Volume measures
are given in cups, millilitres and fluid ounces. Oven
temperatures are given in Gas marks, as well as degrees
Celsius and degrees Fahrenheit. Conversion tables can be
found at the back of the book.

Times, temperatures and quantities are guidelines only.
Personally, I hardly ever measure or time things when I'm
cooking. From practice, I know when things are about right.
(This means that my dishes come out slightly different each
time!) I very rarely follow a recipe exactly myself, so I don't

expect anyone to be exact with my recipes. Use the recipes to get a feel for using the different ingredients. The idea of this book is that you should become confident in using alternatives for foods that you can't eat. Feel free to adjust the quantities to suit your own tastes. There are blank pages for you to add your own recipes and notes.

Soda Bread and Other Loaves

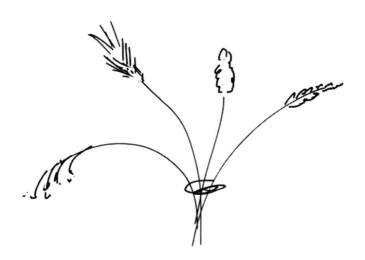

Soda Bread and Other Loaves

The food most people miss most on changing to a gluten free diet is bread. You can buy gluten free bread mixes for use in normal bread recipes, with yeast. These make very nice bread, but as many people with food sensitivities have a problem with yeast it is best to avoid it. Soda bread uses baking soda to make the loaf rise. It won't rise as much as a loaf with yeast, especially if it's gluten free, but it's a reasonable substitute for normal bread. You can still have your toast for breakfast!

You can use the shop gluten free bread mixes in the following soda bread recipe, but check the ingredients carefully. These mixes often contain potato flour, which is fine for many people. If, like me, you have to avoid potato as well as gluten, choose from the gluten free flours listed above. Experiment with different combinations to find what you like best.

I use the same basic method for plain and flavoured soda bread, vegetable or herb loaves and for cakes. (Note: all the following recipes work perfectly well with spelt flour or ordinary wheat flour, if you want to bake for people not on a gluten free diet.)

Plain Soda Bread

INGREDIENTS

500g/18 oz mixed gluten free flour (e.g. rice, gram and buckwheat in
  equal amounts.)

Pinch of salt

2 tsp baking powder*

1 tbsp oil

~ 1 cup/225ml/8 fl oz water

* Don't buy ready-made baking powder as it may contain wheat flour.
  Combine two parts cream of tartar to one part bicarbonate of soda.
  This is pure baking powder without any additives.

METHOD

Preheat oven to gas mark 6, 200°C, 400°F. Grease a loaf tin.
Mix all dry ingredients. Make a well in the centre, add the oil
and water and mix thoroughly, adding more water if
necessary to make fairly wet dough. Pour into the baking tin
and put in the oven. Takes approximately 30 minutes,
depending on how well done you like it. Test with a skewer
as you would a cake. The loaf will be quite crumbly because
it doesn't have gluten in. Tapioca starch helps to hold it
together better. It will be nicest fresh from the oven, or
toasted, as when it's cold the starches are hard – particularly
if it contains maize flour.

Flavoured Soda Bread

There are many possibilities. Try these suggestions, and then make up your own.

Spices – Add a teaspoonful or two of cumin, garam masala, pepper or your own favourite. Mix the spices thoroughly into the flour before adding any liquids.

Herbs – Add one or two teaspoons of dried, powdered mixed herbs (e.g. rosemary, sage, marjoram and thyme) to the dry ingredients *or* make an infusion of dried mixed herbs (i.e. pour boiling water on the herbs and leave to brew, like tea.), strain the liquid, allow it to cool and use the liquid in place of some of the water in the basic recipe. If you want to use fresh herbs, chop them finely and add them to the dry ingredients. Use only small amounts of most herbs, but parsley can be used like a vegetable – use a generous handful at least.

Cheese – If you can eat cheese, you can make a cheese loaf by adding grated cheese to the dough last thing.

Scones

These are basically the same as soda bread, but shaped as scones. Use rice flour for dusting the work surface and rolling pin. You can add any of the usual ingredients (e.g. cinnamon, cheese if ok, or raisins).

Vegetable Loaf

Make the dough as for plain soda bread, and then add chopped or grated vegetables – one or two cupfuls are about right. Most vegetables are suitable e.g. onions, carrots, celery, broccoli, garlic. If you use a lot of vegetables you might want to reduce the amount of flour. This loaf will take longer to cook than plain soda bread, and will be a bit moist when cooked, because of the vegetables. You can add an egg if you want. It will help it hold together better, but it's not essential. Cooked lentils can be added, with the vegetables, for extra protein. A vegetable and lentil loaf makes a main dish for a vegetarian meal.

Notes

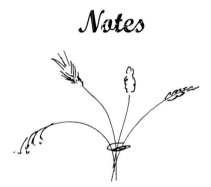

Notes

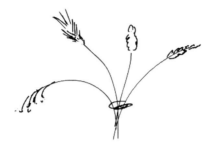

Notes

Cakes

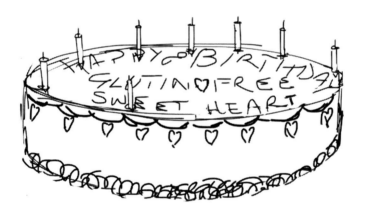

Cakes

Start with the basic soda bread recipe, add one or two eggs and sugar or honey, reduce the amount of flour, and soda bread becomes cake. If you don't use egg it will be less rich, so use a bit more oil, margarine or butter to make up for it, and more baking powder. I always add a small pinch of salt, even in sweet recipes: it brings out the flavours of the other ingredients and helps to balance the richness of sugar and fat.

You can serve these cakes hot as puddings, with custard, chocolate sauce or similar. If you like them as cakes decorate with a suitable icing when cold. Try the recipes and see what you think.

If you decrease the amount of flour and increase the amount of sugar, you will get a lighter cake. Of course, the more sugar you use the less healthy the cake.

I include here my recipe for sugar-free, Chocolate Flavour Cake Topping, which goes very well with Chocolate Cake. You can also make a cake topping with margarine, honey or light brown sugar, and vanilla essence.

General method:

Preheat oven to gas mark 5, 190°C, 375°F. Grease a loaf tin. Mix all dry ingredients (e.g. flour, sugar. cocoa, spices) Make a well in the centre, add the liquid ingredients (e.g. oil, egg, water, honey) and mix thoroughly, adding more water if necessary to make a fairly wet batter. Stir in any other ingredients (e.g. dried fruit, grated or mashed fruit or vegetables). Pour into the baking tin and put in the oven. Takes 30 to 45 minutes, depending on ingredients and how well done you like it. Test with a skewer. (Push a skewer into the centre of the cake; if it comes out clean the cake is done.)

Chocolate Cake

INGREDIENTS

100g/4 oz rice flour

100g/4 oz buckwheat flour

150g/5 oz sugar (preferably brown sugar – the darker the better)

50g/2 oz cocoa

50g/2 oz carob flour

3 tsp baking powder

Pinch of salt

½ tsp cinnamon and/or nutmeg (optional)

1 or 2 eggs

1 tbsp sunflower oil

~1 cup/225ml/8 fl oz water

Carob flour is the ground up beans of the carob tree. They're also known as locust beans. (These are the 'locusts' that John the Baptist lived on 2000 years ago, rather than the grasshoppers, which are probably not so tasty.)

Carob flour is sweet, so that you need less sugar than without it. It's also caffeine free. Carob is also a mild laxative – useful for children who don't eat enough vegetables!

If you want to sweeten the cake with honey, molasses or concentrated apple juice instead of sugar, just add these with the water and oil.

METHOD
Follow the general method.

Banana Cake

200g/7 oz rice flour

50g/2 oz maize flour

2 tsp baking powder

Approx. 50g sugar *or*

3 tbsp honey*

Pinch of salt

½ tsp ground cinnamon

½ tsp grated nutmeg

¼ tsp allspice

1 tbsp sunflower oil (or other light oil)

Water

2 or 3 bananas, mashed

*Sugar goes with the dry ingredients; honey with the 'wet'.

Banana cake is a good way of using up overripe and bruised bananas. The more bananas you use the less sugar you need. It also depends on taste. I prefer to train my children to get used to as little sugar as I can get away with. They all enjoy my cakes, even when I've used barely any sweetening. If you can't use maize, use gram flour instead.

METHOD

Follow the general method, adding the mashed banana last.

Chocolate and Prune Cake

INGREDIENTS

150g/5 oz rice flour

50g/2 oz buckwheat flour

2 tsp baking powder

Pinch of salt

75g/3 oz carob flour

50g/2 oz cocoa powder

2 tbsp molasses

6-8 prunes (soaked overnight or stewed for about half an hour)

1 tbsp sunflower oil

Water

METHOD

Make sure there are no stones in the prunes before pureeing in a food processor. Follow the general method. Add the pureed prunes with the molasses, oil and water. (Use the water that the prunes were soaked/stewed in.)

The prunes and molasses give this cake a strong flavour. Warning: The combination of prunes, molasses and carob makes an effective laxative; so don't eat too much at once!

Carrot Cake

INGREDIENTS

200g/7 oz rice flour

50g/2 oz maize flour

50g/2 oz tapioca flour

3 tsp baking powder

Pinch of salt

½ tsp cinnamon

¼ tsp nutmeg

¼ allspice

100g/4 oz sugar

1 tbsp sunflower oil

1 or 2 eggs (optional)

Water

2 or 3 medium carrots, finely grated

METHOD

Follow the general method. Add the carrot at the end. Eggs make the cake richer and more 'cakey' in flavour and texture.

Sugar-Free Cake Topping

This can be used to ice cakes or as a chocolate spread for gluten-free bread or crackers.

INGREDIENTS

125g/4½ oz non-hydrogenated vegetable margarine *or* coconut oil

45g/2 oz carob flour

25g/1 oz cocoa powder

METHOD

Combine all ingredients until an even consistency is obtained. Adjust proportions to taste. No sugar is needed because both the carob and the margarine have their own sweetness, as does coconut oil.

Note: if your room is quite warm, coconut oil will be liquid. That makes it easier to mix, but you can always put it in the fridge for a few minutes till it sets again.

Flourless Chocolate Cake

This gluten-free chocolate cake has no flour, using ground almonds instead. It is not egg-free, but you could try it using egg-replacer (available in shops) instead of egg. It is a rich, moist cake.

INGREDIENTS

2 eggs plus 2 egg whites

100g/4 oz ground almonds

100g/4 oz butter or dairy-free margarine

150g/5 oz sugar

50g/2 oz cocoa

2 tsp baking powder

METHOD

Preheat the oven to gas mark 6, 200°C, 400°F. Mix dry ingredients. Separate the eggs and beat the egg yolks; melt the butter and add the melted butter and the egg yolks to the dry ingredients. Whip the four egg whites until soft peaks form and fold into the rest of the ingredients. The mixture will be quite wet. Pour into a greased cake tin and bake for approximately 25 minutes. The cake will not rise much and will still be quite moist when done. Makes a rich and tasty cake.

Notes

Notes

Notes

Savoury Recipes

Savoury Recipes

This selection of (mainly vegetarian) recipes for main meals and savoury snacks should give you an idea of the variety of dishes you can make with gluten-free alternatives to wheat and other gluten-containing grains. Some of them contain eggs, but there are egg-free versions for those who need to avoid them.

There's always a way of making a gluten free version of any dish you would normally make with wheat, and there are alternatives to milk and cheese. It's just a matter of getting used to working with the different ingredients. For example, the main ingredients of traditional lasagne are wheat pasta, cheese, tomato sauce and meat. Here you'll find a version without wheat, cheese, tomato or meat – which has been approved by people on 'normal' diets as well as those who live gluten-free, dairy-free.

Use these recipes to get a feel for cooking with buckwheat flour, rice flour, gram flour, etc. Then experiment. There's plenty of space to add your own creations on the blank pages at the end of the section.

.

Vegetable Pancakes 1

INGREDIENTS

100g/4 oz gram flour

100g/4 oz rice flour

Salt to taste

Spices

1½ cups/350ml/12 fl oz chopped or grated fresh herbs or vegetables

A little oil for cooking

METHOD

Mix dry ingredients, add sufficient water to make a batter, mix in the herbs/vegetables. Pour the mixture into a hot, oiled frying pan and spread it roughly, to about ½" thickness.

When it's beginning to dry on top, turn it over. This can be baked in the oven instead of frying. Serve as a side dish, with a salad as a light meal or cut into bite size pieces as nibbles. Choose your own favourite savoury spices. I like coriander, cumin and black pepper. Vegetables could be leeks, broccoli or cabbage finely chopped, or grated carrot and chopped parsley. Use whatever you've got in the fridge or garden. If you want a richer flavour and more protein you can add an egg to the batter.

Vegetable Pancakes 2

The same, but with buckwheat flour instead of rice and gram flours. The colour and flavour are quite different. Try both and see which you prefer.

Corn Pancakes

INGREDIENTS

100g/4 oz maize flour

100g/4 oz rice flour

½ tsp salt

Approx. 1¾ cups/400ml/14 fl oz hot water

Oil or butter for frying

METHOD

Mix dry ingredients. Add boiling water; stir thoroughly to form stiff dough. Use extra rice flour to dust your hands so that the dough doesn't stick to them. Knead for several minutes. It's very important to knead the dough sufficiently while it's hot, otherwise it won't hold together. Take a small ball of dough and roll to a circle about 6″ across (again use extra rice flour to dust the work surface and rolling pin). Fry in a very hot frying pan for one or two minutes each side. Keep them warm by wrapping them separately in tea towels until you're ready to serve them. Can be served with salad, baked beans, etc – or just a dab of butter.

This method of mixing the flour with hot water works with some other flours, particularly the more starchy ones. Try using tapioca starch or arrowroot with other gluten free flours.

Buckwheat Pancakes 1 *(with egg)*

INGREDIENTS

1 egg

Water

A few tbsp buckwheat flour

Pinch of salt

Oil or butter for frying

METHOD

Beat egg with a little water. Gradually mix in the flour to form a thin batter. Pour a little at a time into a hot, oiled, frying pan. Tip the pan to spread the batter evenly. (Don't use too much oil.) Buckwheat pancakes are traditionally served with maple syrup, but they're very nice savoury – add your favourite spices to the flour. (I like cumin with buckwheat.)

Buckwheat Pancakes 2 *(without egg)*

As above, but use just water instead of egg and water. It doesn't hold together so well, but it still works if you're careful.

Gluten-Free, Dairy-Free Lasagne 1
(with meat)

INGREDIENTS

Gluten free lasagne pasta (available from health food shops and some
supermarkets.)

'Notcheese sauce' (see recipe)

Meat sauce:

2 tbsp olive oil

2 onions

2 cloves garlic

1 lb mince beef

Pinch dried mixed herbs

1 400g/14 oz tin tomatoes

2 tbsp tomato puree

Salt and pepper to taste

METHOD

Peel and finely chop the onions. Heat the oil in a saucepan
and gently fry the onion until beginning to soften. Add the
mince beef and the garlic, crushed. Continue frying, stirring
constantly, until the meat is just browned. Add the remaining
ingredients, cover and simmer gently for about 45 minutes.
Heat the oven to gas mark 5/190°C/375°F. Assemble the
lasagne in six layers as follows: put half the meat sauce in the
bottom of a lasagne dish, cover with a layer of gluten-free
lasagne pasta, then half the 'notcheese' sauce. Repeat the
layers. Bake until the top just begins to brown.

Gluten-Free, Dairy-Free Lasagne 2
(without meat)

INGREDIENTS

Gluten free lasagne pasta

'Notcheese sauce' (see recipe)

Vegetarian sauce:

2 medium onions

2 cloves garlic

2 medium carrots

1 stick celery

1 400g/14 oz tin tomatoes

1 tbsp tomato puree

200g/7 oz red lentils

Pinch dried herbs

Salt and pepper to taste

2 tbsp olive oil

Approximately 2 cups/450ml/16 fl oz water

METHOD

Peel and chop the onions. Place in a pan with the olive oil and begin to cook over a low heat. Peel and mince the garlic, chop the carrots and celery. Add these to the pan with the onions. Cook until the onions are beginning to soften. Add the tinned tomatoes, tomato puree, lentils and water. Put the lid on the pan, bring to the boil and simmer until the lentils are soft. (A pressure cooker saves a lot of time here.) While the sauce is cooking preheat the oven to gas mark 5/190°C/375°F. If the sauce is too wet, strain off some of the liquid. Use the sauce as it is if the vegetables are in suitably small pieces, or puree for a smoother texture.

Assemble lasagne layers in the usual way, i.e. a layer of vegetable sauce, a layer of gluten free pasta, a layer of 'Notcheese' sauce, and repeat. Place in the oven and cook until the top begins to brown.

SMELLS GOOD

Gluten-Free, Dairy-Free Lasagne 3
(without meat or tomatoes)

Tomatoes have a texture, colour and flavour that are hard to imitate. The 'Mock Tomato' sauce below goes some way to replacing the texture and sweetness of a tomato sauce. Use it in the recipe above for vegetarian sauce instead of the tomatoes and tomato puree. Assemble the lasagne as usual, i.e. a layer of vegetable sauce, a layer of gluten free pasta, a layer of 'Notcheese' sauce, and repeat. Bake in a moderately hot oven (gas mark 5/190°C/375°F) until the top just begins to brown.

Mock Tomato Sauce

This recipe makes a really good sauce. Your family won't believe there's actually no tomato in it! The small piece of beetroot gives it the 'tomato' colour. The other secret ingredient is a dried apricot, which gives a sweet tang to the flavour.

INGREDIENTS

2 medium onions

2 medium carrots

½ sweet potato

½ a small parsnip

1 clove garlic (optional)

I small piece of beetroot

1 dried apricot (preferably unsulphered)

Salt and pepper

1 tbsn olive oil

METHOD

Peel and chop the vegetables. Put the oil in a saucepan and sauté the onions with the lid on till they begin to soften. Chop the beetroot and dried apricot very small. This is especially important for the apricot, otherwise you may end up with chewy lumps that won't blend properly. Add all the other ingredients, with sufficient water and cook till the carrots are soft.

Blend the sauce really well. You want a really smooth texture.

You can leave out the parsnip if you don't like it, but it does make for a creamier texture. If you don't have sweet potato, use an extra carrot.

This sauce can be used anywhere you'd normally use tomato sauce – e.g. in lasagne, or with spaghetti, with or without meat. You can vary it by adding more or less water. If you make it quite thick (less water) you can use it as a pizza topping. Add more water and you can serve it as soup. I've served this 'Mock Tomato' soup to people who say they only like tinned tomato soup, and they've liked it – and even asked for seconds!

Savoury Crumble

INGREDIENTS FOR THE CRUMBLE TOPPING

50g/2 oz millet flakes

75g/3 oz rice flour

50g/2 oz ground nuts or seeds

  (e.g. almonds, sunflower seeds, hazels)

Herb salt or celery salt

Pepper

Spices (e.g. cumin, Garam Masala)

Oil

INGREDIENTS FOR THE FILLING

A selection of seasonal vegetables e.g.

onions, carrots, leeks, broccoli, parsnip,

peas, beans.

(Sufficient quantities to fill a casserole dish about 2/3 full.)

METHOD

Preheat the oven to gas mark 5/190°C/375°F.

Prepare the vegetables as normal, chopping into fairly small pieces. Place in a saucepan with a little olive oil. Fry gently until the onions are beginning to soften. Add water and simmer, covered, until the vegetables are just cooked. While the vegetables are cooking, prepare the topping: combine all dry ingredients and add enough oil to make a crumbly texture.

Put the cooked vegetables in a casserole dish, pressing them down slightly with the back of a spoon. Cover with the crumble mixture and place in the oven to bake until the topping is just beginning to brown.

SMELLS GOOD

Polenta

INGREDIENTS

1 cup/225ml/8 fl oz polenta meal (coarse maize meal)

3 cups/675ml/24 fl oz water

2 tbsp olive oil

Salt to taste

METHOD

Place all ingredients in a saucepan. Heat gently, stirring all the time, until the mixture is thick (rather like porridge). Stir in the olive oil. Pour the mixture into a deep baking tray and leave to set for 6 to 8 hours. Cut into slices and fry, or bake in the oven (gas mark 5/190°C/375°F, 20-30 minutes) before cutting and serving.

There are many variations on plain polenta. You can add herbs, spices or vegetables to the mixture. As polenta is an Italian dish, courgettes, olives, tomatoes and sweet peppers are particularly suitable.

Gram Flour Polenta

This is cooked in the same way as ordinary polenta (see previous recipe), but uses gram flour instead of maize meal. Use approximately 2 cups (450 ml/16 fl oz) of water to 1 cup of gram flour.

CHICKPEAS

Lentil Burgers

INGREDIENTS

150g/5 oz green lentils (soaked overnight)

2 small onions

1 or 2 cloves garlic, crushed (optional)

Buckwheat flour, approximately 1 heaped tbsp

1 cup/225ml/8 fl oz chopped herbs (e.g. parsley, chives) and/or finely
    shredded, leafy vegetables (e.g. cabbage, kale)

Salt and pepper to taste

Oil for frying

METHOD

Cook the lentils in plenty of water (at least one pint/600 ml)
till soft. (A pressure cooker saves time for cooking pulses and
grains.) Chop the onions finely and fry gently till soft (with
the garlic, if used). Drain excess water off the lentils.
Combine all ingredients, using just enough buckwheat flour
to make the mixture stick together. Too much flour and it
will be crumbly. Taking a large spoonful at a time, form into
burgher shapes in your hands or between two spoons. Fry on
both sides till just beginning to crisp on the outside. When
cooked, these burgers hold together well and even look rather
like beef burgers in colour and texture. Makes approximately
12 small burgers.

Millet Patties

INGREDIENTS

1 cup/225ml /8 fl oz millet (whole grains)

3½ cups/800ml/28 fl oz water

Salt

Pepper

1 egg

Garlic (optional)

1 bunch parsley

Oil for frying

METHOD

Cook the millet in the water till soft; leave it to cool while preparing the other ingredients. Beat the egg; add salt and pepper to taste. If using garlic crush it finely before adding. Chop the parsley finely. Thoroughly combine all ingredients in a large mixing bowl. Taking a tablespoonful at a time, form the mixture into patties and fry gently. You may need to push the mixture together as it cooks. When one side is beginning to crisp, turn carefully and cook the other side. You can make these without egg, but it's tricky to get them to stick together. Don't try to turn them too soon – once one side is cooked they hold together better.

Spicy Sweet Potato Dip

INGREDIENTS

½ onion

1 medium sweet potato

½ -1 tsp curry powder or chilli powder

Olive oil

Salt to taste

METHOD

Fry the spice gently in a little olive oil for a minute, before adding the chopped onion. Fry till the onion is soft. Peel and finely dice the sweet potato. Place all ingredients in a food processor and blend until smooth. Serve as a dip with sticks of carrot, celery, gluten-free pastry etc; or use as a spread on gluten-free bread or toast.

Note: Yes, the sweet potato is raw. If you prefer, you can cook it with the onion.

Variations: use other vegetables and other spices to make a selection of dips. Most root vegetables will work – e.g. carrots or beetroot. Try a combination of raw and cooked onion. Add a little honey and vinegar for a sweet and sour dip. Mix in some chopped herbs – chives, mint, parsley or sorrel for example. Use the following blank pages to make notes on your experiments with different ingredients.

Stuffed Mushrooms

This recipe needs a bit of forward planning as the nuts and seeds need pre-soaking. You can vary the recipe by using different nuts and seeds, or by adding herbs or spices.

INGREDIENTS

125g/4½ oz almonds

125g/4½ oz sunflower seeds

2 tbsp olive oil

Juice of ½ lemon

½ tsp salt

Water

Medium cup mushrooms, as fresh as possible

METHOD

Soak the almonds and seeds in cold water for at least four hours, or overnight. Drain the water from the nuts and seeds, and then place in a food processor or blender with the oil, lemon juice and salt. Process until smooth adding fresh water a little at a time as necessary. Remove the stalks from the mushrooms and spoon the nut mixture on top of each. Serve as a starter or as finger food for a party.

This nut mixture can also be used as a dip or a spread.

Tabouleh Salad

Tabouleh salad is a Middle Eastern dish traditionally made with cracked wheat (bulghar wheat). Quinoa makes an ideal substitute. This is an extremely healthy salad, very rich in vitamins and minerals. It's also delicious. (If you can't eat tomatoes, just leave them out.)

INGREDIENTS

2½ cups/575ml/20 fl oz Quinoa, cooked and cooled

1½ cups/350ml/12 fl oz finely chopped parsley

¾ cup/175ml/6 fl oz finely chopped fresh mint leaves

3 medium tomatoes

3 spring onions

1 clove garlic (or more, if liked)

Lemon juice (up to ½ cup/125ml/4 fl oz)

¼ cup/50ml/2 fl oz olive oil

Salt and pepper to taste

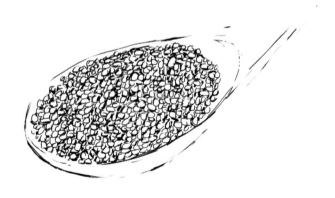

METHOD

Mix the dressing of olive oil, lemon juice, salt and pepper.
Add crushed garlic. Chop the tomatoes and spring onions
finely. Add all ingredients and mix thoroughly.

Notes

Notes

Notes

Pastry

(SMELLS GOOD)

Pastry

Gluten-free pastries are a little tricky to work with compared with wheat pastry, being rather crumbly and brittle. Experiment with various combinations of gluten free flours. Use rice, buckwheat and gram flours in various proportions. Maize flour can be used if it is suitable for your diet. Ground sunflower seeds add richness and help the pastry hold together better. Tapioca flour is also very good for making the pastry a little less crumbly. Some recipes for gluten-free pastry include egg. This certainly improves the consistency, but is not suitable for everyone.

I use sunflower oil for baking, but you can use any light vegetable oil or dairy-free, non-hydrogenated vegetable margarine instead. Coconut oil is good if you like the flavour.

Try my recipes, and then experiment with different ingredients and different proportions. Use the following blank page to record your own favourite combination.

Vegetable Pie

INGREDIENTS

FOR THE PASTRY

250g/9 oz rice flour

50g/2 oz gram flour

50g/2 oz buckwheat flour

100g/4 oz ground sunflower seeds

Pinch of salt

Sunflower oil

Water

FOR THE FILLING

2 onions

2 carrots

1 medium sweet potato

½ swede

1 cup/225ml/8 fl oz cooked butter beans

METHOD

Preheat the oven to gas mark 6/200°C/400°F approx.

Grease a pie dish.

For the filling: Peel and dice the vegetables, and place in a saucepan with a little olive oil. Fry gently until the onions are beginning to soften. Add water and simmer, covered, until the vegetables are just cooked. For children (and adults) who won't eat vegetables, use a food processor to blend the vegetables with the beans until smooth, using as little water as possible. It's surprising what they'll eat if they don't recognise it!

For the pastry: Combine all dry ingredients, add the oil and mix thoroughly. Add sufficient water to bind the mixture, without it being too wet to handle. For a pie base, rather than roll out the pastry and try to lift it, place a lump of pastry into the pie dish and press it into shape with your hands. (Dust your hands with rice flour.) Place the filling in the pie, draining off as much liquid as possible.

To make the pie 'lid', roll out the pastry to a slightly larger size than you need. Don't roll it too thin or it will easily become hard when cooked. Cut the pastry into halves or quarters and lift one section at a time onto the pie, using a spatula to support it. Overlap the sections to completely cover the pie, and brush the edges with water to stick them together. The pastry is very brittle and you will probably have to patch it a bit, but once cooked the texture and flavour are good.

Vegetable Pasties

Make the pastry and the filling as for the vegetable pie. Roll out the pastry and cut into 6" squares, put a little of the filling in the centre of each square and fold in half to make a triangle. Brush the edges of the pastry with water to stick. Use a spatula to lift each pasty carefully on to a greased baking tray. You can add cheese to some of the pasties, depending on individual tastes and diets. Be sure to mark the cheese ones, perhaps with a bit of cheese on top.

Bake until the pastry is just firm but not too hard (about 20 minutes for a pie, less for smaller pasties).

Apple Pie

INGREDIENTS

250g/9 oz rice flour

100g/4 oz tapioca

100g/4 oz gram flour

Pinch salt

2-4 cooking apples

Handful of sultanas (optional, but adds sweetness)

½ tsp cinnamon

Pinch nutmeg

METHOD

Preheat oven to gas mark 6/200°C/400°F.

For the pastry, follow the instructions given for vegetable pie (above). Peel and cut the apples. Fill the pie base with apple a little at a time adding spices and sultanas as you go. Make the pastry lid (see instructions under vegetable pie) and bake until the pastry is firm.

Celery Straws

These are a dairy free alternative to cheese straws, flavoured with celery and spices. They make a good snack food on their own, or can be served with a dip.

INGREDIENTS

100g/4 oz rice flour

100g/4 oz gram flour

100g/4 oz ground sunflower seeds

2 tbsp sunflower oil

3 stalks celery

¼ tsp cumin

¼ tsp coriander

Salt

Pepper

METHOD

Preheat the oven to gas mark 5/190°C/375°F. Grease a baking tray.

Mix all dry ingredients and add the oil. Finely grate the celery. What you'll get is mostly liquid once you've removed the long fibres. Add this to the pastry mixture with enough water to bind it. Roll it out directly onto the greased baking tray. (Use a little extra rice flour to dust the rolling pin.) Use a knife to mark it into straws about an inch wide. Cook for approximately 10 minutes.

Notes

Notes

Notes

Desserts

Desserts

While a lot of desserts are dairy based or made with wheat flour, there is still plenty of choice for those on gluten free, dairy free diets. Try fruit salad, stewed fruit, sorbets and jellies. The gluten-free cakes mentioned above could all be used for desserts, and of course, apple pie (under PASTRY, above). Below are a few other dessert ideas, including two different recipes for gluten-free apple crumble. There are blank pages for your own ideas.

Apple Snow

INGREDIENTS

1 large cooking apple

White of two eggs

¼ tsp cinnamon

Sugar to taste

METHOD

Peel and chop the apple. Cook in a little water until soft. Whip the egg whites until they are stiff. Add cinnamon and sugar to the apple and fold into the egg white. Serve immediately.

Apple Crumble 1

INGREDIENTS

100g/4 oz millet flakes

100g/4 oz rice flour

50g/2 oz soft brown sugar

½ tsp grated nutmeg

1 tsp cinnamon

Pinch of salt

2 tbsp sunflower oil

2 or 3 large cooking apples

METHOD

Preheat the oven to gas mark 6/200°C/400°F approx. Mix all the dry ingredients, add the oil and mix well. Peel and slice the apples. Place the sliced apple in an ovenproof dish; pour the crumble evenly over the top. Bake for about 25 minutes (until beginning to brown on top.)

This makes a very tasty crumble. Plenty of cinnamon and freshly grated nutmeg means that the crumble topping has lots of flavour without the need for much sugar. Compare this crumble to one made with white (wheat) flour and lots of white sugar in the crumble and on the apple – much healthier!

To make the apple crumble sweeter without using more sugar use dessert apples or dual-purpose apples instead of cooking apples.

Apple Crumble 2

INGREDIENTS

1 cup/225ml/8 fl oz almonds

1 cup/225ml/8 fl oz sunflower seeds

1 cup/225ml/8 fl oz hazels

Grated nutmeg

Cinnamon

Soft brown sugar

2 or 3 large cooking apples

METHOD

Preheat the oven to gas mark 6/200°C/400°F approx. In a food processor or coffee grinder, process the almonds, sunflower seeds and hazels until finely ground. Add in the cinnamon and sugar. Prepare the apples as normal and cover with the nut mixture. Bake until the topping is just beginning to brown.

Both these crumble toppings can of course be used with rhubarb or any other suitable fruit.

Gluten-Free (Chocolate) Shortbread

INGREDIENTS

100g/4 oz butter or non-dairy margarine

50g/2 oz caster sugar

50g/2 oz rice flour

25g/1 oz cocoa powder (optional)

Pinch of salt

Extra rice flour for rolling out dough

METHOD

Cream together the butter, or margarine, and sugar. Add all the dry ingredients. Mix well until you have a smooth dough.

Chill the dough in the fridge for half an hour. Before removing the dough from the fridge, preheat the oven to gas mark 4/180°C/350°F. Using extra rice flour to dust the work surface and rolling pin, roll out the dough and place on a baking tray. (Alternatively, roll the dough directly on the baking tray.) Bake for 10 minutes. When done cut into squares and cool on a wire rack.

Kuzu Apple Pudding

This delicious pudding is actually a medicine, being very healing for many digestive disorders.

INGREDIENTS

1 cup/225ml/8 fl oz apple juice

2 tbsp Kuzu starch

1 tsp vanilla extract

1 tbsp tahini

METHOD

Put the apple juice, kuzu and vanilla in a small saucepan and stir until the kuzu has dissolved. Heat gently, stirring constantly, until it has thickened. Stir in the tahini. If you can't eat tahini (sesame paste) leave it out or substitute with a nut butter that you can use (if there is one). Serve hot or cold. These quantities are for one person. Increase quantities as required for more people.

Egyptian Sweets

No cooking required for these healthy sweets!

INGREDIENTS

50g/2 oz dried figs

100g/4 oz dates

50g/2 oz almonds

50g/2 oz sunflower seeds

METHOD

In a food processor or coffee grinder, grind the nuts and seeds finely. Add in the dried fruit and process till there are no large pieces. The mixture should stick together. If it doesn't, you may need a little more dried fruit. Taking a spoonful at a time, shape into balls. You can roll the balls in a little extra ground almonds, or in desiccated coconut.

There are many variations possible here. You can use almost any dried fruits and almost any nuts or seeds. You can add vanilla essence or spices such as cinnamon, nutmeg or cardamom. A little honey can be added (reduce the quantity of dried fruit proportionately). For a nut free version, try using rice flour instead of ground nuts or seeds (you might need to add a little oil or margarine). The following is a chocolate-flavoured version.

Dairy Free Chocolate Truffles

Again, no cooking required for this delicious treat.

INGREDIENTS
50g/2 oz cocoa powder
25g/1 oz carob flour
75g/3 oz dates
75g/3 oz sultanas

METHOD
Put all the ingredients in a food processor and process until the mixture sticks together. Form into balls and roll the balls in cocoa powder.

If it doesn't seem to hold together well, you might need to add a little more dried fruit – some dried fruit is drier than others.

Variation: if you've got time to plan ahead you can soak the dried fruit for a few hours (or overnight) and use a blender to puree them with the soak water – make sure there are no stones. Then stir in the carob and cocoa.

More variations: using the soaked fruit method it's very easy to add other ingredients. My family particularly like these sweet treats with desiccated coconut. You could also try ground almonds or other nuts. Try adding a drop of vanilla or mint essence, or your favourite spice, for a different flavour.

Notes

Notes

Notes

Milk and Cheese Substitutes

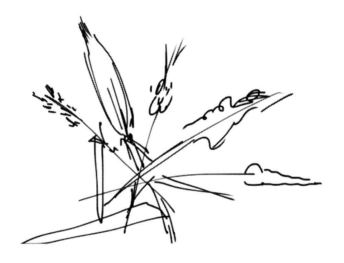

Nut Milk

½ cup/125ml/4 fl oz nuts or seeds (almonds, hazels, cashews,
  sunflower or sesame seeds are all suitable)
1½ cups/350ml/12 fl oz water
A little honey
Cinnamon, nutmeg or vanilla essence to flavour

METHOD

Using a food processor, grind the nuts as finely as possible.
Blend the ground nuts with the water, honey and spices. You
can strain the mixture through a fine sieve if you prefer a
smoother drink. The pulp can be saved to add to cakes for a
bit of extra protein.

This is a basic recipe. You can make many different flavours
by adding, for instance, banana, figs, dates, lemon juice or
apple. Different combinations of nuts or seeds will give more
subtle variations of flavour.

Cashew Cream

This recipe is ready in minutes and makes a delicious creamy sauce that can be used in sweet or savoury dishes. I like to use it as a vegan substitute for mayonnaise. It also makes a great dip – add chives or other flavours, or serve it as it is. Cashew cream can be used as a dairy free alternative to sour cream – leave out the pepper and use just a tiny pinch of salt.

INGREDIENTS
75g/3 oz cashew nuts
Juice of ½ lemon
¼ cups/50ml/2 fl oz water
2-3 tbsn olive oil
Salt and pepper to taste

METHOD
Grind the cashew nuts to flour in a food mill, coffee grinder or food processor. Put all ingredients in a blender jug and blend till smooth.

It will keep in the fridge for two or three days. It will thicken with time as the cashew flour soaks up the water.

Notcheese Sauce

INGREDIENTS

2 medium onions

1½ cups/350ml/12 fl oz cooked chickpeas

100g/4 oz plain tofu (optional)

1 tbsp miso

Seasonings (e.g. pepper, cumin)

Oil for frying

METHOD

Chop the onions roughly and fry them in a little oil till soft. (You can add garlic if you like.) Place all ingredients in a food processor and blend until smooth.

This sauce can be used for Cauliflower cheese, Lasagne, Welsh Rarebit or anywhere else you would normally use cheese sauce. You can even try it for a substitute for cheese on pizza. It forms a nice crispy, brown crust when grilled or baked. The colour is quite good, but you can add a little turmeric if you want it more yellow.

You can use sprouted chickpeas instead of cooking them. They are more nutritious this way, but you have to plan ahead a day or two. As an alternative to chickpeas, you can use butterbeans or navy beans. Other beans have too strong a colour; the sauce won't look like cheese sauce.

Nut and Seed "Cheese"

This uses wheat grains in the preparation, but it is gluten-free. It is made using the liquid from soaking whole-wheat grains (wheat berries) for sprouting. The cheese is fermented and contains 'good' bacteria such as found in yoghurt. It takes several days in total to make because the grains have to be soaked for 24 hours.

INGREDIENTS
Water
1 cup/225ml/8 fl oz wheat grains
1 cup/225ml/8 fl oz blanched almonds
1 cup/225ml/8 fl oz sunflower seeds
4 or 5 spring onions
Salt to taste
Pinch of dried mixed herbs

METHOD
Put the grains in a bowl with 3 cups of water, cover and leave for 24 hours. Drain the liquid off and reserve. Grind the nuts and seeds finely in a food processor. Chop the spring onions finely. Using 1 cup of water from the sprouted grains, combine all ingredients in a mixing bowl. The mixture will be fairly sloppy, but cover it with a clean cloth and leave it in a warm place for 6 to 12 hours, stirring once or twice. The result is a food of a soft texture and a delicious taste that can

be used as a spread or dip. You can try other flavours, for instance garlic and parsley instead of spring onion and mixed herbs.

Nut cheese will keep in the fridge for several days.

Note: gluten is not water-soluble, so there will not be any gluten in the water drained off the wheat sprouts. The sprouts can be used to make Essene bread (not gluten free) or sown to grow wheat grass (which is gluten free).

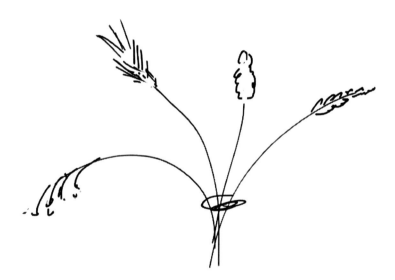

Notes

Notes

Notes

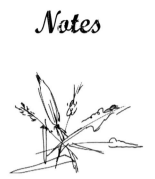

Conversion

Tables

Weights and Measures

I've given measurements in metric and Imperial. To keep numbers simple, the following equivalents have been used. (As one ounce is actually just over 25 grams, these are not exact conversions, but will give the right proportions for cooking if you use either metric or imperial.)

Metric g	Imperial oz
25	1
50	2
75	3
100	4
125	4 ½
150	5
175	6
200	7
250	9
300	10 ½
350	12
400	14
450	16 (1lb)

Spoon measurements are all metric:
1 level teaspoon (tsp) = 5 millilitres (ml)
1 level tablespoon (tbsn) = 20 millilitres (ml)

For liquid measures, approximate equivalents are given below for millilitres (ml), fluid ounces (fl oz) and cups.

ml	fl oz	Cups
25	1	1/8
50	2	¼
75	2 ½	
100	3	3/8
125	4	½
150	5	5/8
175	6	¾
200	7	7/8
225	8	1

Oven Temperatures

These are approximate equivalents for gas mark, degrees Celsius (°C) and degrees Fahrenheit (°F). Remember that ovens vary.

Gas mark	°C	°F
1	140	275
2	150	300
3	160	325
4	180	350
5	190	375
6	200	400
7	220	425
8	230	450
9	240	475

Index of Recipes

GOOD THINGS TO EAT

Recipes

The Author

Caroline Osborne was born in London, where she spent the first eleven years of her life. Her parents then immigrated to Perth, Australia where she and her four brothers and sisters spent the rest of their childhood.

Caroline studied science at the University of Western Australia, before working for two years in research for the Australian Government.

When she returned to London she began her study of alternative medicine and natural health.

She is married with six children and lives in Norfolk.

Caroline can be contacted through her website, www.glutenfreedairyfree.co.uk.

Lightning Source UK Ltd.
Milton Keynes UK
UKOW02f0151100316

269912UK00001B/15/P